4/14

Everyday Science Experiments

Bubbles in the Bathroom

Susan Martineau
Illustrated by Leighton Noyes

with thanks to Kathryn Higgins,
Head of Chemistry, Leighton Park School

WINDMILL
BOOKS
New York

Published in 2012 by Windmill Books, An Imprint of Rosen Publishing
29 East 21st Street, New York, NY 10010

© 2012 b small publishing ltd
Adaptations to North American Edition © 2012 Windmill Books, An Imprint of Rosen Publishing

Library of Congress Cataloging-in-Publication Data

Martineau, Susan.
Bubbles in the bathroom / by Susan Martineau. — 1st ed.
p. cm. — (Everyday science experiments)
Includes index.
ISBN 978-1-61533-371-4 (library binding) — ISBN 978-1-61533-409-4 (pbk.) —
ISBN 978-1-61533-471-1 (6-pack)
1. Water — Experiments — Juvenile literature. 1. Title.
GB662.3.M365 2012
507.8 — dc22
2010052117

Manufactured in the United States of America

CPSIA Compliance Information: Batch #BS2011WM: For Further Information contact Windmill Books, New York, New York at 1-866-478-0556

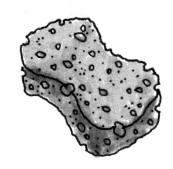

Contents

How to Be a Scientist

Scientists learn about the world around us by doing experiments. This book is full of experiments you can do in your bathroom. You won't need any special equipment. You'll probably have everything you'll need at home already. Remember to ask a grown-up before using anything. Before you begin, always read through the whole experiment to make sure you have everything you will need.

BE SAFE!
Never play with the medicines or cleaning products you might have in your bathroom.

Bubble Fun

A bubble bath is lots of fun. Have you ever wondered how those soapy bubbles are made? This experiment shows you how they form.

1. Fill a sink halfway with water.

2. Pour a bit of bubble bath into the water.

3. Put a straw into the water and blow!

6

Let's Take a Closer Look!

When you blow into the water, you make loads of bubbles. The bubble bath makes the water elastic, or stretchy, so that it holds the air you are blowing into it. If you blow into water without the bubble bath, the water on its own cannot hold the air.

Did You Know?

Your skin never stops growing. When you wash yourself, soap loosens dirt from the skin and also washes away some dead skin. You might find that your fingertips feel smoother after washing your hands!

Always wash your hands after going to the bathroom to wash off any germs.

7

Misty Mirrors

You can do this experiment the next time
you take a bath or shower.
It'll make getting clean more fun!

1. Shut the
bathroom door.
Don't lock it,
though!

2. Run a
nice warm
bath or
shower.

3. Watch what
happens to the
windows and
mirrors in the
bathroom.

Let's Take a Closer Look!

The warm bath or shower water gives off a **gas** called **water vapor**. This water vapor is made when the **liquid** bath water is warmer than the air in the room. When the water vapor touches something cold, such as a mirror or window, it turns back into liquid drops again. This is called **condensation**.

Quick Warning!
Always be very careful when running hot water. Ask a grown-up to help you.

Don't leave the faucets dripping. This wastes water.

Quick Quiz!
Can you think of another word for water vapor?

Try This!
Breathe hard on a cold mirror and see what your warm breath does to it.

A Magic Cup

This is a great trick to play on your friends and family. They really won't believe it! Use a plastic cup. That way you won't have to worry about dropping it.

1. Fill the cup halfway with water.

2. Put a piece of stiff cardboard over the top of the cup.

3. Hold the cardboard firmly in place and turn the cup upside down.

4. Take your hand away from the cardboard.

Do this experiment over the bathtub or sink!

Let's Take a Closer Look!

Air all around us is pushing up, down, and sideways on everything it touches. This is called **air pressure**. The air pushes up on the cardboard, too. It pushes up more strongly than the air inside the cup pushes down. This is why the water does not fall out.

Quick Fact
The air inside your bicycle tires pushes back, too. That's why they can carry your weight as you ride along.

Try This!
Blow up a balloon. If you press your hand against it, you can feel the air inside it pushing back.

Float a Boat

How do boats manage to float on the top of water instead of sinking? In this experiment, you are going to make one and find out. You need two balls of modeling clay.

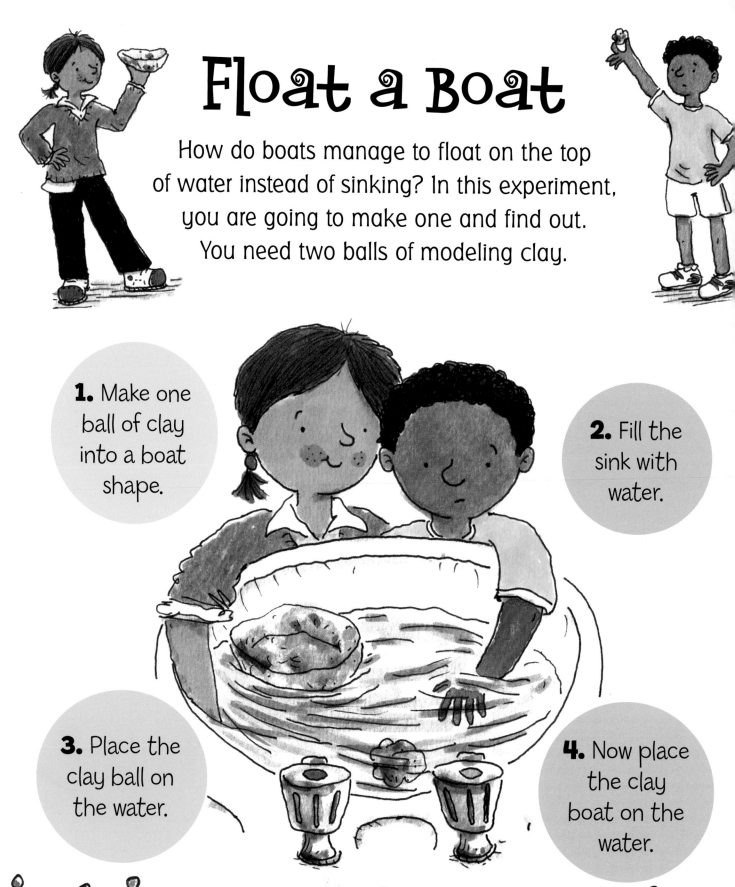

1. Make one ball of clay into a boat shape.

2. Fill the sink with water.

3. Place the clay ball on the water.

4. Now place the clay boat on the water.

Let's Take a Closer Look!

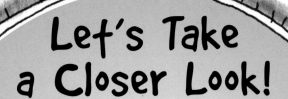

The ball of clay sinks to the bottom. The boat floats, though. The boat stays on the **surface** of the water because there is air between the sides of it. This makes it light for its size. The ball has no air inside it. It is heavy for its size, so it sinks.

Quick Quiz!

Do you think a toothbrush will sink or float?

Try This!

See if other things in the bathroom float or sink in the water. You could try bottles of shampoo, bars of soap, and toothbrushes.

Write or draw which things sink or float in your notebook.

Water Fights Back

You will need an empty shampoo or bubble bath bottle for this experiment. You can do it in the bathtub instead of a sink if you like.

1. Put the lid on the bottle. Fill the sink with water.

2. Lay the bottle on the top of the water.

3. Let the bottle float on the water.

4. Now try to push the bottle down under the water.

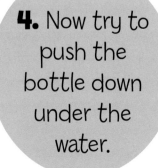

A Greek scientist called Archimedes did experiments like this in his bath, too!

Let's Take a Closer Look!

Like the boat on page 12, the bottle is lighter than the water and so it floats. When you push the bottle down into the water, it pushes the water out of the way. However, the water pushes back. This is why it is difficult to push the bottle down under the water.

Did You Know?

Since our bodies are lighter than water, we can float like the bottle. When you are in the ocean or the swimming pool, the water is also pushing up against you and helping you to float.

Quick Fact

Deep-sea divers have to wear heavy weights to keep the water from pushing them up!

Toothbrush Trick

Light can play some funny tricks on our eyes. This experiment will show you a light trick with a toothbrush.

1. Fill a clear, plastic cup halfway with water.

2. Put your toothbrush into the cup.

3. Look at the toothbrush through the side of the cup.

Quick Quiz!

Will the toothbrush look bent if you put it in the cup without water?

Try This!

Next time you go swimming, stand in the pool and look down at your legs. They look short and stubby because of refraction.

Let's Take a Closer Look!

The part of the toothbrush under the water looks bent. Light moves more slowly through water than through air. As the light slows down, it changes direction and enters your eyes from a different angle. This is why things in water look bent even though they are really straight. It is called **refraction**.

Don't forget to brush your teeth twice a day!

17

Squeeze and Squirt

This experiment will probably spray a lot of water all over the place, so do it over the bathtub! You'll need two empty shampoo or bubble bath bottles.

1. Take the caps off of the bottles and fill them with water.

2. Put the cap back on one of the bottles, leaving the lid open.

3. Hold one bottle in each hand and squeeze them both hard!

Did You Know?

A faucet has one big hole for the water to come out. However, a showerhead has lots of small holes in it so that the water shoots out with more power.

Have a towel ready to mop up any water!

Quick Fact

Taking a quick shower uses up less water than taking a bath.

Let's Take a Closer Look!

When you squeeze the bottles, you make the water come out. The bottle with the cap on it squirts the water much farther. This is because the water is being forced through a much smaller hole than it is in the bottle with the cap off.

19

Plug Power

Have you ever watched what happens to the water when you pull the plug out of the bathtub or sink? This experiment shows you what happens.

1. Put the plug in the sink. Fill the sink with water.

2. Float a piece of toilet paper on top of the water.

3. Pull the plug out and watch the toilet paper.

Don't forget to take the toilet paper out of the drain!

Let's Take a Closer Look!

When you take the plug out of the sink, the water does not go straight down the drain. Instead it swirls around. This swirling is called a vortex. It makes the toilet paper turn around as the water drains.

Did You Know?

The Romans did not have toilet paper like us. They used sponges on sticks instead. Yuck!

Quick Quiz!

Why must you wash your hands after going to the bathroom?

21

Wrinkly Skin

You might have noticed that your hands and feet get all wrinkly when you stay in the bath or a swimming pool for a long time. Why does this happen?

1. Take a good look at your hands and feet.

2. Run yourself a nice, warm bath.

3. Sit in the water for at least 15 minutes.

4. Look closely at your hands and feet.

Let's Take a Closer Look!

Your fingers and toes have gotten all wrinkly. Our skin has a special oil in it that keeps water from soaking into it. This makes it almost completely waterproof. If you keep your hands and feet in water for a while, this oil washes off. Your skin soaks up some water and gets all wrinkly.

Don't worry. Your skin will go back to normal very soon!

Quick Fact

You can live for weeks without food but only a few days without water.

Try This!

Drip some water onto your arm. You will see that the water drops run off. They don't soak in because the oil in your skin makes it waterproof.

READ MORE

Fulcher, Roz. *Science Around the House: Simple Projects Using Household Recyclables.* Mineola, New York: Dover Publications, 2010.

Mason, Adrienne. *Change It!: Solids, Liquids, Gases and You.* Primary Physical Science. Tonawanda, New York: Kids Can Press, 2006.

GLOSSARY

air pressure (EHR PREH-shur) The weight of the air.

condensation (kon-den-SAY-shuhn) Cooled gas turning into drops of liquid

gas (GAS) Matter that has no set shape or size.

liquid (LIH-kwed) Matter that flows.

refraction (rih-FRAK-shun) When something, such as a light ray or sound wave, is bent away from a straight path.

surface (SER-fes) The outside of anything.

water vapor (WAH-ter VAY-pur) Water that is a gas.

Quiz Answers

Page 7 – Shampoo
Page 9 – Steam
Page 13 – It will sink.
Page 17 – No, it will look straight.
Page 21 – To clean off germs.

INDEX

WEB SITES

For Web resources related to the subject of this book, go to: www.windmillbooks.com/weblinks and select this book's title.